Imagine. . .

Exploring Israel

Marji and Micheal Gold-Vukson • Kar-Ben Copies, Inc.

To Aunt Pearl
With Love

Cover Art by Leeann Lidz

my name _____

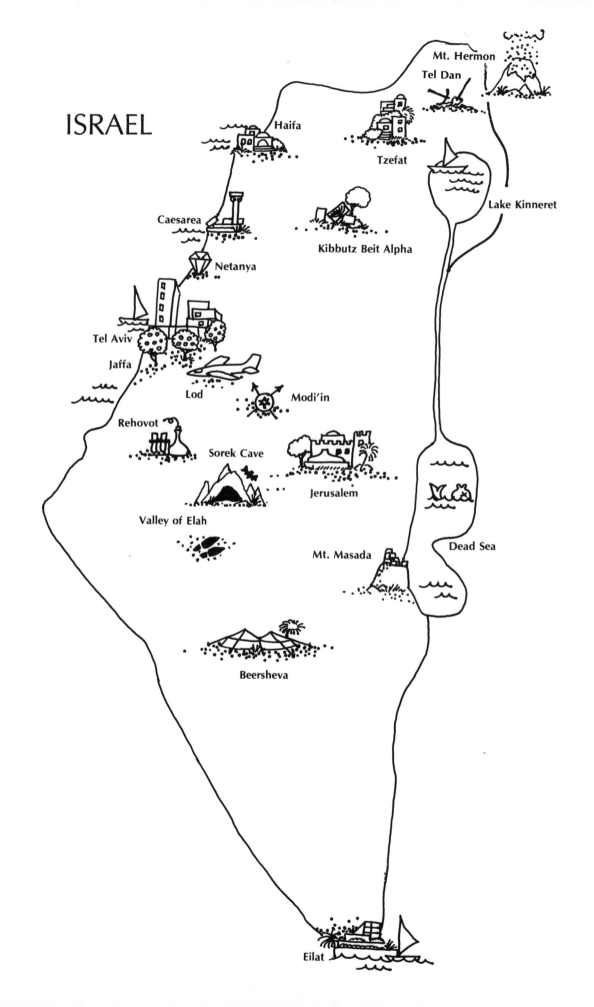

ISRAEL

Mt. Hermon

Tel Dan

Haifa

Tzefat

Lake Kinneret

Caesarea

Kibbutz Beit Alpha

Netanya

Tel Aviv

Jaffa

Lod

Modi'in

Rehovot

Sorek Cave

Jerusalem

Valley of Elah

Mt. Masada

Dead Sea

Beersheva

Eilat

CONTENTS

En route 6
Lod 7
Jerusalem
    Kotel 8
    Hezekiah's Tunnel 9
    Hadassah Medical Center 10
    Yad Vashem 11
    Biblical Zoo 12
Egged Bus 13
Sorek Cave 14
Modi'in 15
Tel Aviv
    Museum of the Disapora 16
    Dizengoff Circle 17
Factories 18
Jaffa 19
Netanya 20
Caesarea 21
Haifa 22
Jezreel Valley 23
Kibbutz 24
Lake Kinneret 26
Tzefat 28
Tel Dan 29
Mt. Hermon 30
Conservation 31
Valley of Elah 32
Rehovot 33
Beersheva 34
Dead Sea 35
Masada 36
Eilat 38
My Hat 40
Photograph 41
Souvenir 42
Yom Ha'atzmaut 43
Centennial 44
Eretz Yisrael 45
Encouraging Artistic Expression 46
About the Authors 48

En route: It takes many hours to fly from North America to Israel. Passengers eat, sleep, read, play cards, and even watch movies during the flight. Can you think of something *different* to do on the plane?

Lod: Each day, many planes land at **Ben-Gurion Airport's** busy international terminal. What do you think passenger aircraft will be like when you're grown? Draw a plane of the future at the El Al gate below.

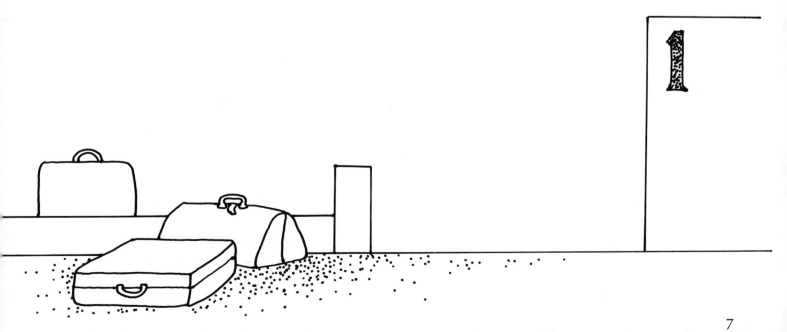

Jerusalem: Once, the Holy Temple was here. Today, only a piece of the Western Wall, the **Kotel** still stands. People from all over the world come here to pray. Some write prayers on small pieces of paper to slip between the stones. Draw your own prayer to tuck into the Wall.

Jerusalem: Hezekiah's Tunnel was built almost 3,000 years ago to connect the water source of Gihon Spring to the Siloam Pool. The tunnel is more than a quarter of a mile long. Suppose that you entered the tunnel at the Gihon end and someone (or something) unusual entered at the Siloam end. Show your encounter.

9

Jerusalem: Artist Marc Chagall created 12 beautiful, stained-glass windows for the **Hadassah Medical Center Chapel** in the Jerusalem Hills. They tell us about the Twelve Tribes of Israel. Design a new window for the Medical Center.

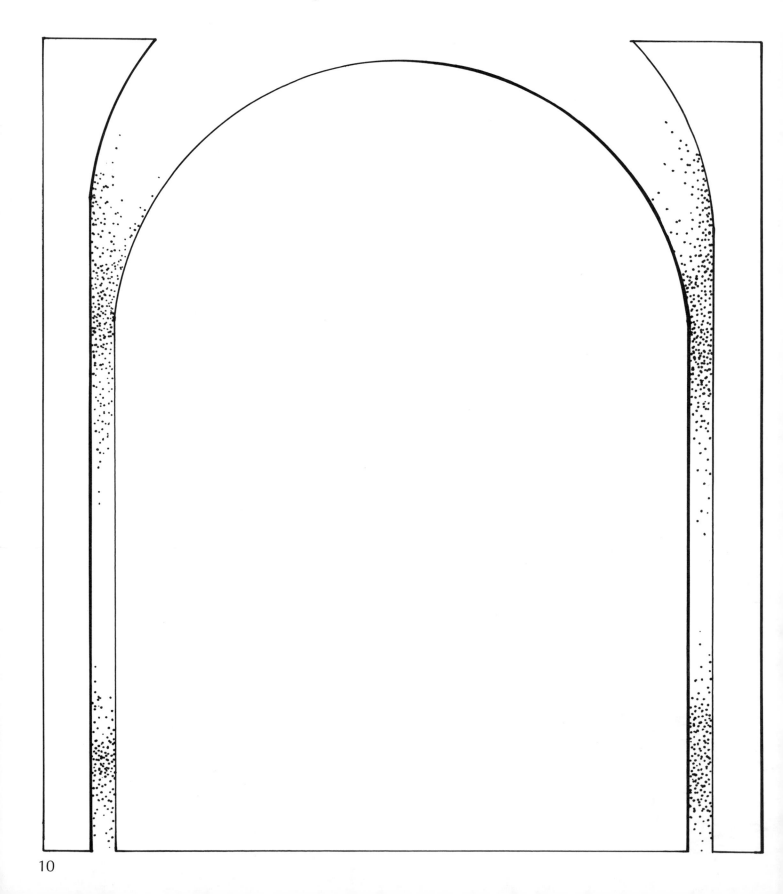

Jerusalem: The Avenue of the Righteous, leading to **Yad Vashem**, is lined with trees honoring brave non-Jews who helped Jews during the Holocaust. Suggest another way to honor these unselfish heroes.

Jerusalem: At the **Biblical Zoo**, you will find almost all of the 100 animals and 30 birds named in the Bible. A sign on each cage tells the name of the animal and the chapter and verse where it is mentioned. Design an unusual travel poster about the Biblical Zoo.

The Egged Bus is a great way to get from town to town in Israel. Pretend that one day something very unusual boarded the bus you were riding. Draw what happened next.

The Sorek Cave, which covers an area of over 15 acres in the Avshalom Nature Reserve, is the largest cave in Israel. It is famous for its spectacular stalactites and stalagmites. One rock formation reminded you of something funny! Draw it.

Each Hanukkah, we tell the story of brave Judah Maccabee and his tiny band of Jewish patriots, who fought for freedom against the mighty Syrians. The Maccabees came from **Modi'in** where today, you can see a reconstructed village from that time. If you were designing a stamp to honor Judah Maccabee, what would it look like?

15

Tel Aviv: A wonderful place to learn about Jewish life *outside* Israel is at the **Museum of the Diaspora** *inside* Israel. Dioramas, models, photographs, films, and computers tell the story of thousands of years of world Jewish history. Suppose your life was the subject of a museum exhibit. Show what the display would look like.

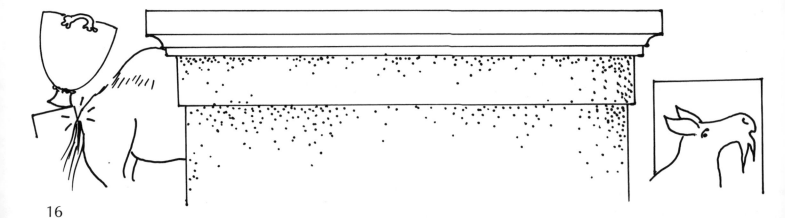

Tel Aviv: At **Dizengoff Circle**, you can shop, splash your feet in the sparkling fountain, or sit under a huge umbrella at an outdoor cafe and eat felafel. But, that doesn't look like felafel! What strange things did you put in that pita, anyway?

Factories in Israel make machinery, electronics, clothing, metals, and food. Many advertise their wares at bus stops throughout the country. Design a bus stop billboard to advertise your factory's product.

Sweet, juicy oranges that grow in Israel's orchards are exported from the busy port of **Jaffa** to countries all over the world. Invent a silly new machine that can pick, peel, and serve fresh Jaffa oranges.

At **Netanya's** many diamond factories, you can watch workers cut and polish millions of dollars worth of gems right before your eyes! Design a new piece of diamond jewelry.

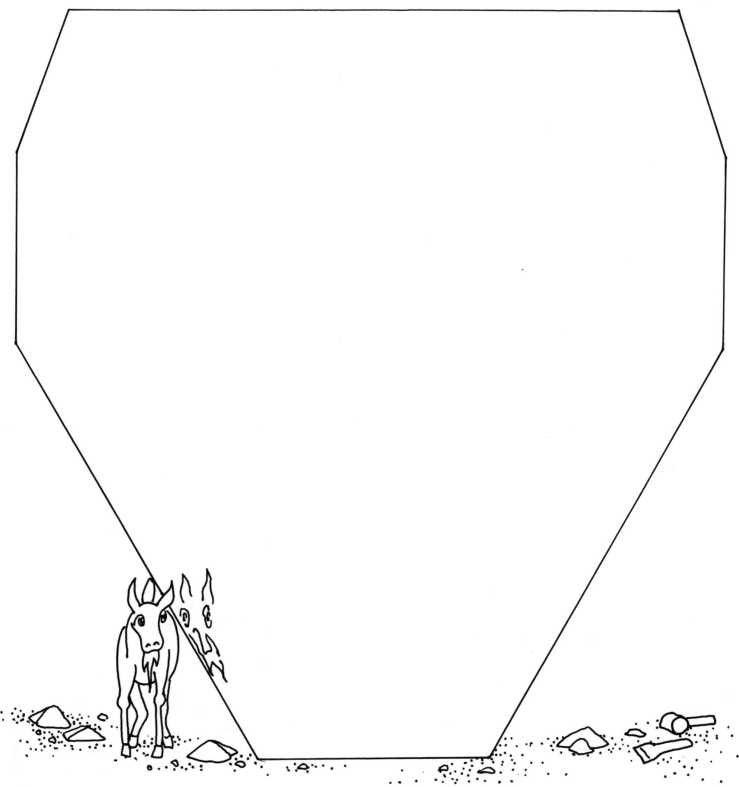

When King Herod built **Caesarea** many centuries ago, he created "The Street of Statues" to honor famous Roman rulers. Who would you choose to honor today? Design a new statue to put on the street.

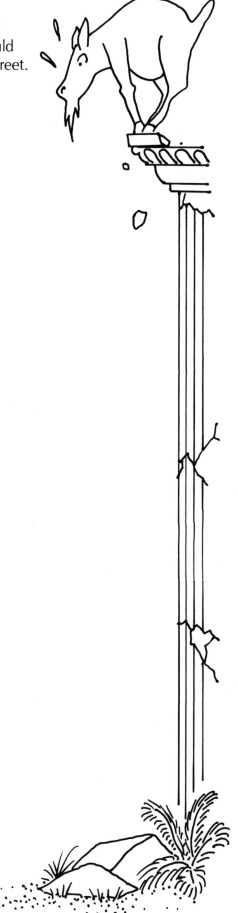

Haifa's busy harbor is where luxury liners, oil tankers, and Navy ships all dock. Some of the crates below will be loaded onto cargo ships. Others were just unloaded. Show what might be in each one.

Jezreel Valley: Kibbutz Beit Alpha has a beautifully preserved mosaic synagogue floor. Pictures made of tiny pieces of stone and glass show the Holy Ark, Zodiac signs, and the story of Abraham and Isaac. What shapes and pictures would you include in a mosaic floor?

If you lived on a **kibbutz**, you would receive your housing, food, clothes, and other necessities in exchange for the work you do for the community. You might work in an orchard or factory, in a barn or school. Show the job you would most like to have.

עבודה

Design a map showing what your **kibbutz** looks like. Include the family apartments, office, playgrounds, children's zoo, dining hall, laundry, air raid shelter, orchard, water tower, cow barn, factory, and swimming pool. Are there any other buildings on your kibbutz?

Lake Kinneret (Sea of Galilee): To make Israel's dusty, brown desert bloom, water from Lake Kinneret in the north is pumped all the way down to the Negev desert through the canals and pipelines of the National Water Carrier. Can you draw another creative way to get water to the desert?

Suppose you were fishing in **Lake Kinneret**. . .and caught something really astonishing. Show what you caught.

"Look out!" That's the meaning of **Tzefat**, Israel's highest city. Perched on the side of a mountain in the Upper Galilee, Tzefat is famous for its Artists' Quarter. Painters and sculptors enjoy working in the bright, hilly countryside overlooking Lake Kinneret. If you were an artist in Tzefat, what might you paint?

Tel Dan is one of over 3,500 sites in Israel where archaeologists have found coins, pieces of pottery, jewelry, and utensils buried in the ruins of ancient cities. Pack your compass, pick, shovel, and pail and join a "dig." Sketch something unusual and important you discovered.

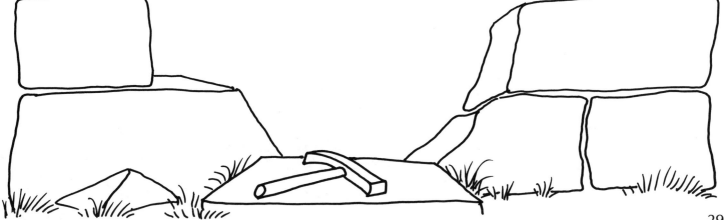

Mt. Hermon, Israel's tallest peak, is covered with colorful flowers in the spring, but later in the year, it becomes a snowy winter wonderland. What if there were a snow sculpting contest on Mt. Hermon? Show the 1st, 2nd, and 3rd place winners.

Conservation is important to Israel. The country boasts impressive nature reserves, miles of hand-planted forests, and the Hai-Bar program which brings the animals of the Bible back to Israel. Design a conservation poster that reminds people to help out.

The Valley of Elah is where the story of David and Goliath took place. There are no giant footsteps in the valley today, but you can see a kibbutz and a satellite receiving station. Have you ever faced a "giant" problem of your own? Use pictures to tell about it.

Some cities in Israel make us think of the past. **Rehovot** makes us think of the future. At the Weizmann Institute of Science, researchers study computers, lasers, atomic particles, and more! If you worked at the Institute, what would your laboratory look like?

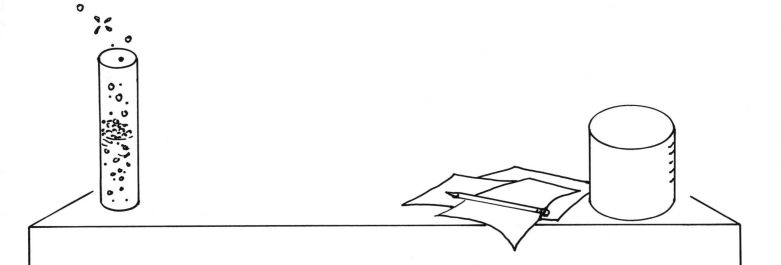

Bedouin families move from place to place in the sandy Negev desert. Some live in tents all year long. On Thursdays, the Bedouins bring camels, sheep, goats, and other products to sell at the market in **Beersheva**. Draw some of the more unusual things they are selling.

The Dead Sea got its spooky name because it is so full of salt and natural chemicals that fish and other sea creatures can't live in it. The water is so thick that no one ever sinks! Suppose that one day something very strange and unexpected happened there. Create a cartoon to show what occurred.

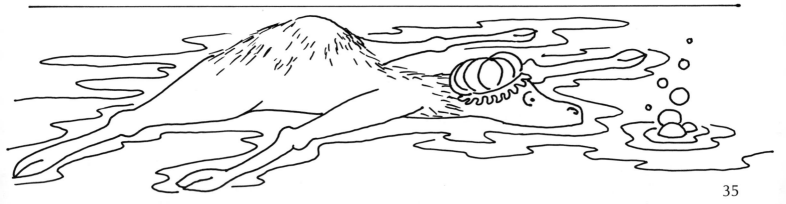

Steep, rocky **Mt. Masada** looms high above the Dead Sea. Long ago, Jews built a fortress there. Today, some visitors hike up a long "snake path" to the top. Others ride up in a cable car. Can you invent a new way to reach the fortress at Masada?

Pretend that archaeologists just uncovered something amazing at **Masada!** Draw it.

In **Eilat**, visitors sail on glass bottom boats in the Red Sea. They watch colorful tropical fish and fancy coral right through the floor! Draw what the most interesting fish and sea creatures might look like.

Now, draw what the fish would see when they looked back at the tourists through the glass bottom of the boat!

Hakova Sheli (My Hat): You can tell a lot about Israelis by the hats they wear. Air Force officers, Greek Orthodox clergy, Islamic court judges, Bedouin women, Druze elders, Hassidim, kibbutzniks, and scouts. . .almost everyone has a special hat. Design a unique hat or cap that best identifies you.

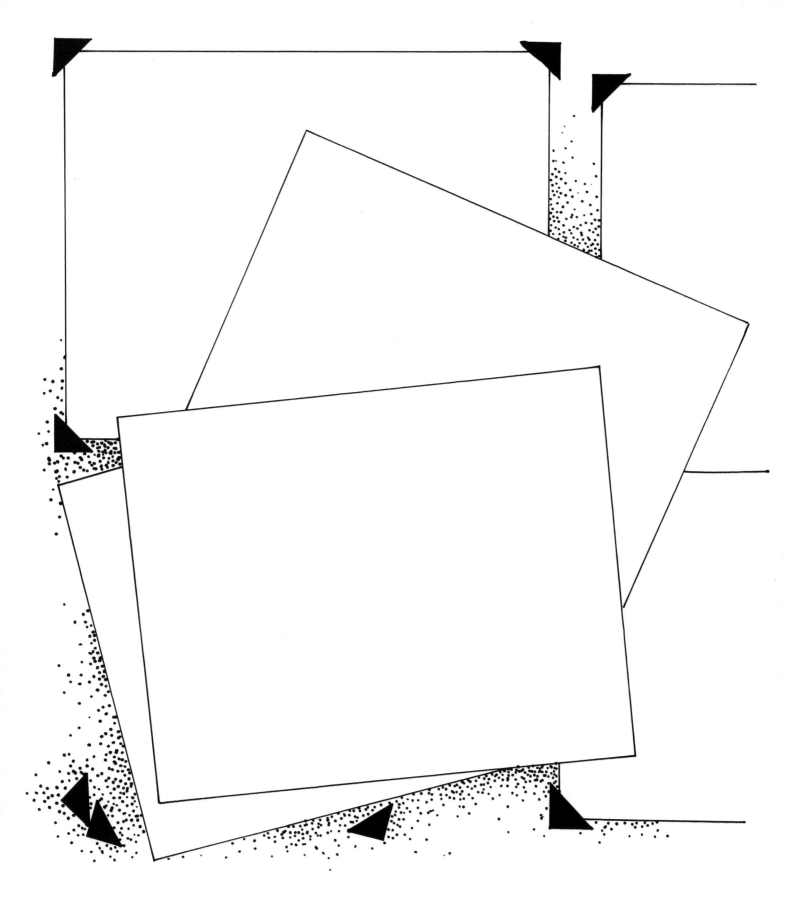

Photograph: You are right to be proud of all the great photographs you took on your trip to Israel! Let's see your favorite picture.

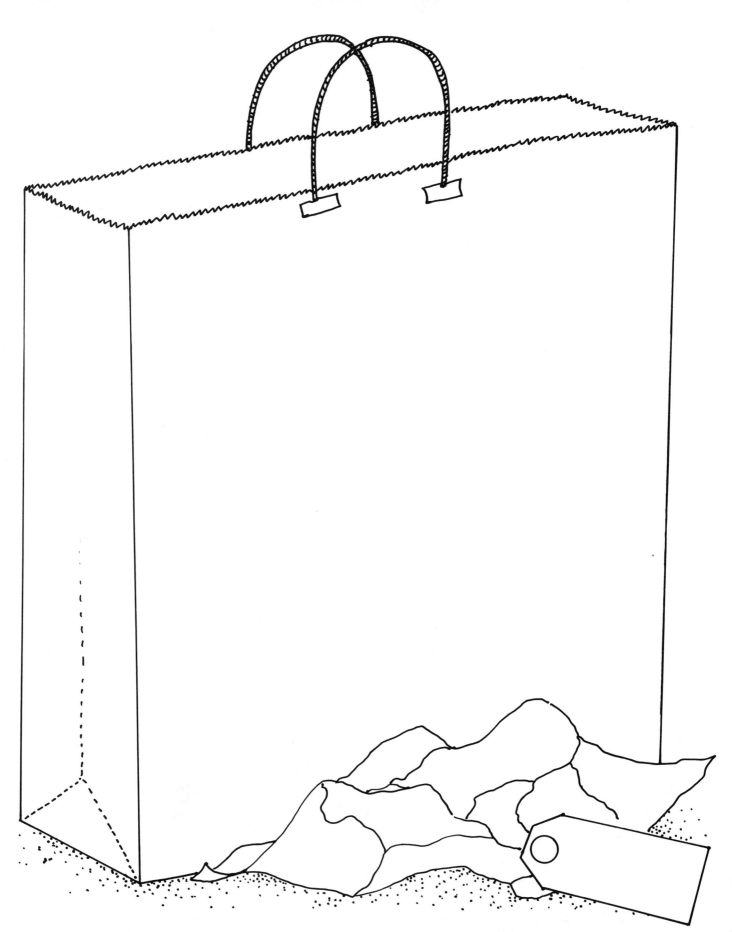

Souvenir: Hurray! You've located the perfect souvenir of your trip to Israel! Show what you've found.

Yom Ha'atzmaut: The 5th of Iyar is Israel's Independence Day! Design a spectacular new float for the Yom Ha'atzmaut parade.

Centennial: The year is 2048—Israel's 100th anniversary. To celebrate, the Israeli government has asked you to design a special commemorative coin. What will it look like?

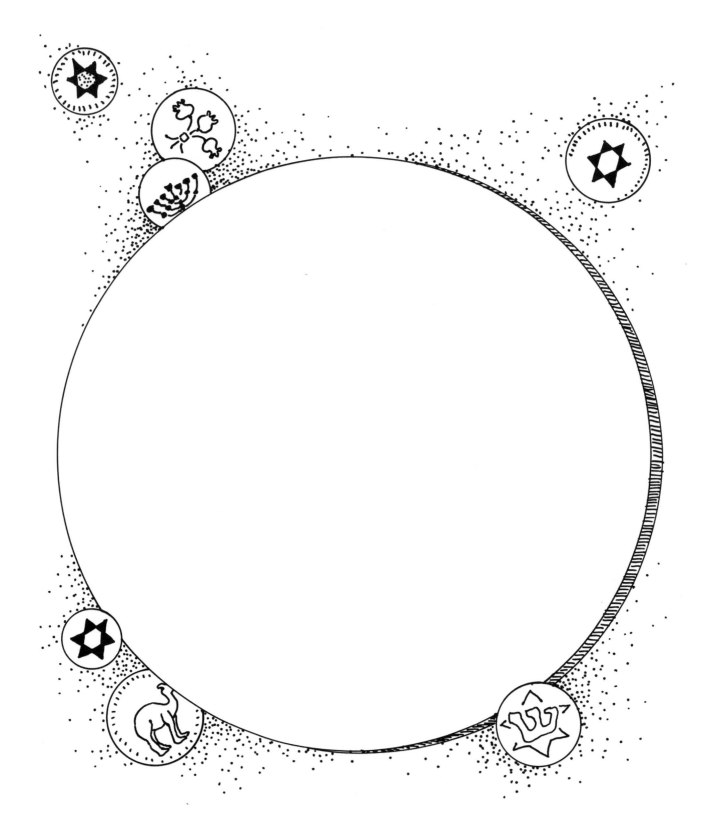

Eretz Yisrael (The Land of Israel): Draw a picture of what you would most like to see and do if you went on a real trip to Israel.

Tips for Encouraging Artistic Expression

1. Foster imagination and new directions of thought. It is important to refrain from imposing adult standards and ideas on children, from interfering with too many questions, and from encouraging great similarity among the products of different children.

2. Allow for experimentation with many different age-appropriate drawing materials:

    Ages 5-8:   crayons (assorted sizes and colors), colored-chalk, felt-tip pens, pencils (regular and colored), ball-point pens

    Ages 8-10: same as above plus charcoal, oil pastels, colored markers

    Be sure to provide work space and plenty of TIME, too.

3. Provide a wide variety of topic-related background experiences, such as holiday stories, films, tapes, songs, speakers, or model ceremonies.

4. Be an enthusiatic role model by showing an interest in both the topic and the art process.

5. Encourage the children to discuss and evaluate their own work. Exhibit the work non-judgmentally.

6. Review your own art background. Feel free to expand upon it and to share what you have learned with your children.

Don't Stop There!
Creative Ways to Expand Upon Drawing Adventures

It's easy to expand upon the drawing adventures in this book! Here are some ideas to help you get started:

Substitute Other Projects for Drawing Activities

Substituting another project for a drawing activity can be as simple as constructing a picture with felt pieces instead of with crayons. Here is a partial list of other projects that can be done by following the directions on an activity page and then using interesting materials to complete the assignment:

> banners, batiks, bulletin boards, bumper stickers, buttons, cartoons, ceramics, collages, comics, designs, diagrams, etchings, films, flannel boards, graphics, illustrations, lithographs, macrame, masks, mobiles, montages, murals, needlework, origami, paintings, papier mache, patterns, pennants, photos, postcards, posters, prints, puppets, quilts, scrapbooks, sculptures, shadow boxes, silk screen, stained "glass" (plastic), string art, tie-dye, triptychs, wall hangings, weavings, and woodwork.

Elaborate Upon Drawing Activities

After completing a drawing activity, use the illustration as a blueprint or basis for other projects. Perhaps the drawing can be the inspiration for a poem or skit. Examples of elaboration might also include:

> advertisements, announcements, articles, audio tapes, ballads, billboards, books, collections, costumes, dances, debates, demonstrations, discussions, displays, drama, editorials, essays, exhibits, flags, games, graffiti, greeting cards, interviews, jingles, jokes, journals, kits, learning centers, letters, lists, models, music, myths, newscasts, oral reports, outlines, pamphlets, parties, quizzes, radio programs, recipes, reenactments, rhymes, simulations, slogans, stories, surveys, tape recordings, transparencies, want ads, and warnings.

About the Author and the Artist

Marji Gold-Vukson was born in Stamford, Connecticut and, by the time she was a senior in high school, had lived in 7 different cities, 12 different houses, and had attended 11 different schools. In more recent years, Marji settled long enough to receive her Masters of Science in Education from Purdue University, to teach elementary public and religious school classes, and to collaborate with her husband, Micheal, on four kids and 16 books.

Micheal Gold-Vukson grew up in Mendota and DePue, Illinois. He is currently completing work on his Ph.D. in Art Education from Purdue University, teaching elementary art classes on the faculty of the Lafayette Indiana School Corporation, and, along with his wife, Marji, is raising four artistically-creative little Gold-Vuksons.